Contents

Introduction

Look closely in a garden and you will find many interesting things. You can have fun learning about creatures and where to find them. Make a worm garden and watch worms at work in the soil. Plot an ant map and attract birds with a bird cake. See what plants need in order to grow and find out who visits the garden when you're not there.

1 Look out for numbers like this. They will guide you through the step-by-step instructions for the projects and activities, making sure that you do things in the right order.

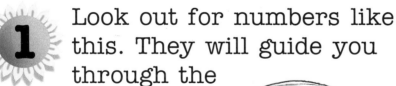

Further facts

Whenever you see this 'nature spotters' sign, you will find interesting information, such as how to recognise animal footprints, to help you understand more about your nature garden.

discovering nature

Nature Garden

Sally Hewitt

Franklin Watts
London • Sydney

An Aladdin Book
© Aladdin Books Ltd 2000
Produced by
Aladdin Books Ltd
28 Percy Street
London W1P 0LD

First published in Great Britain
in 2000 by
Franklin Watts
96 Leonard Street
London EC2A 4XD

ISBN 0-7496-3714-5 (hardcover)
ISBN 0-7496-4611-X (paperback)

Editor: Kathy Gemmell

Consultant: Helen Taylor

Designer: Simon Morse

Photography: Roger Vlitos

Illustrators: Tony Kenyon, Stuart Squires – SGA
& Mike Atkinson

Printed in the U.A.E.

Original concept by David West Children's Books

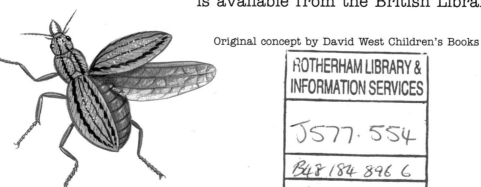

Hints and tips

•When you look for things in the garden, be careful not to tread on any plants.

•Try to look at creatures without disturbing them. If you do move them, always return them to the place where you found them.

•Before touching soil, always cover any cuts you may have with a plaster.

•Do not rub your face or eyes when working with plants or soil. Always wash your hands afterwards.

Wherever you see this sign, ask an adult to help you. Never use sharp tools or go exploring on your own.

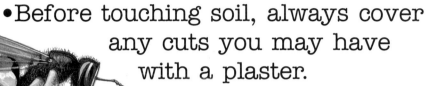

Get an adult to help you

DON'T TOUCH ROTTEN THINGS

This warning sign shows where you have to take special care when doing the project. For example, when looking at rubbish rotting in bags of soil, keep the bags sealed. Don't touch or smell the rotten things. They may give you germs that make you ill.

Soil

Soil is a very important part of your nature garden. It is full of the minerals and water that plants need for growth. Moles, worms and all kinds of tiny creatures make it their home.

Soil settling

1 Find out what makes up the soil in your nature garden. Dig up some soil from the edge of a flower bed and put it in a bucket.

2 Shake some soil in a sieve over the bucket. Sort what is left behind onto some paper. You may find stones, bits of plants or even creatures that live in the soil.

3 Now put some soil into a screw-top jar. Fill the jar nearly to the top with water and screw on the lid.

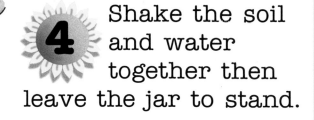

4 Shake the soil and water together then leave the jar to stand.

5 Carefully look at the jar without disturbing it. The soil will have settled down into layers in the water.

Soil layers

Soil is a mixture of dead plants and animals and tiny pieces of broken down rock. Different kinds of rock will make sandy, chalky or sticky clay soil.

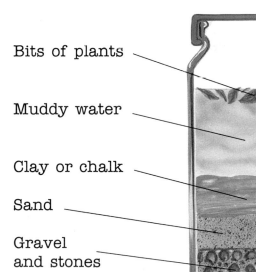

Bits of plants

Muddy water

Clay or chalk

Sand

Gravel and stones

Rotting rubbish

Dead plants and animals that rot down into the soil help to make it rich and good for new plants to grow in. Not everything rots down quickly. Some rubbish stays around for a very long time.

Bags of rubbish

1 See what kind of rubbish rots away and what doesn't. Don't throw away banana skins, apple cores, tissues, cans or crisp packets – bury them!

NEVER TAKE RUBBISH FROM THE BIN

2 Put some soil into clear plastic bags. Push one piece of rubbish into the soil in each bag and seal it.

3 Check the bags every few days, but don't open them. You will see that apple cores rot quickly, but banana skins take a long time. Rubbish made of plastic doesn't rot at all.

 **Natural rotters**

There are many different plants and animals that get to work straight away on natural rubbish like leaves, logs or dead creatures. They are called decomposers.

Fungi are not really plants. They grow and feed on dead wood.

Lichens grow on stone and wood and gradually break them down.

Worms pull leaves and bits of dead plant down into the soil and eat them.

Maggots that hatch from housefly eggs eat the bodies of dead creatures.

Woodlice live in dark, damp places and feed on leaves and wood.

Seeds

Gardeners look after the plants and flowers they want to grow in their garden and spend a lot of time pulling up weeds that they didn't plant. You can discover what seeds are hiding in the soil, waiting to grow.

Soil gardens

1 Dig up some soil from two different places in the garden, perhaps from under a tree and by a fence. Put the soil from each place into its own plastic tray and label where it came from.

2 Water both trays every other day. After a while, you will see shoots beginning to push up through the soil, even though you didn't plant any seeds.

3 Some shoots may become grass or weeds. A seed from a tree may one day grow into a young tree. A rose tree may even grow from a rosehip dropped by a bird.

 **Spreading seeds**

Plants have different ways of spreading their seeds to give them a good chance to grow into new, strong plants.

Birds eat juicy berries, such as cherries. The seeds are stones inside the berry, which fall to the ground in the birds' droppings.

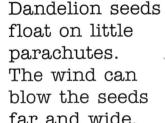 Horse chestnut seeds are heavy and fall straight to to the ground. Look for them under a horse chestnut tree.

Dandelion seeds float on little parachutes. The wind can blow the seeds far and wide.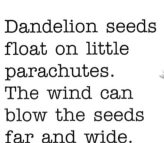

Green grass

Grass in the countryside is food for animals and it is like a soft, green carpet in the garden. Grass has another job to do too.

Grass roots hold soil in place in the wind and the rain. Different kinds of grass grow in different soils.

In the dark

1 This project will show you that sunlight is what makes grass green. Find a corner of your lawn.

2 Cover a patch of grass near the edge of the lawn with a thick piece of card. Put a stone on it to stop it blowing away.

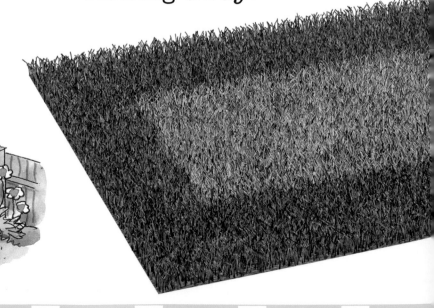

3 Lift up the card after two weeks and see what has happened to the grass. When it is kept in the dark, grass will turn pale green or yellow and begin to die.

Using sunlight

Like grass, other plants also need sunlight to grow and survive. Plants make their own food using sunlight. This is called photosynthesis.

Photosynthesis
Plants need sunlight to make food using the green colour in their leaves, called chlorophyll.

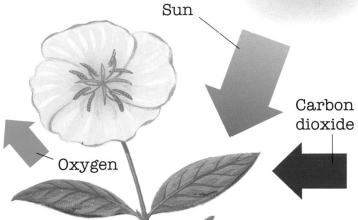

Sun

Carbon dioxide

Oxygen

As part of photosynthesis, plants give out a gas called oxygen.

The green leaves catch the Sun's energy. They use the energy to make food from water and a gas in the air called carbon dioxide.

Without sunlight, plants could not make food and would die.

Plants

We all have veins to carry blood around our bodies. Plants have veins too. They carry the water and minerals a plant needs to grow to every part of it. Watch how water moves up the stem and into the leaves of a celery stalk.

Drinking water

1 For this project you will need a jar of water, some blue food colouring and a celery stalk with leaves.

2 Mix the water and blue food colouring together in the jar and put in the celery stalk. Leave the jar near a window for a few hours.

3 The blue water will slowly rise up the veins in the stalk then into the leaves, turning them blue.

Get an adult to help you

4 Now slice the stalk across the middle. You will be able to see the veins that have been stained blue.

Roots

Roots grow downwards into the soil to hold the plant in place. They have tiny hairs to suck up the water and minerals that a plant needs from the soil. Water goes into the roots, then up the stem into the leaves, then out into the air.

Carrots and potatoes are swollen roots which store food for the plants.

Water in the soil

Flowers

A plant starts life as a tiny egg. Flowers are the parts of a plant where eggs that become seeds are made. The seeds then grow into new plants. If you look closely at a flower, you will see all the parts it needs for making seeds.

Parts of a flower

1 Stamens grow from the middle of the flower. Yellow powder called pollen is made on the tip of the stamens. Pollen gives some people hayfever.

Ovary

Stem

Petal

Pollen

Stamen

2 Petals use colours, patterns and smells to attract insects and birds that feed on pollen and on a sweet juice made by the plant called nectar.

Stamen

Stigma

3 A stigma also grows from the middle of the flower. Pollen grains that land on the stigma grow a tube down to join an egg in the ovary. The egg can then become a seed.

4 The ovary is the case where eggs that become seeds are made.

From stigma

Ovary

Pollen fertilises an egg to make a seed.

Flower power

Look out for flowers of all colours, shapes, sizes and smells growing in different places in the garden.

Apple blossom

Apple blossom on an apple tree becomes fruit in the summer.

Daffodil bulbs can be planted in pots and window boxes.

Daffodil

Honeysuckle grows up walls and fences. It smells very sweet.

Honeysuckle

Birds

Birds are visitors to the garden, looking for food and water. In the spring, they may find a sheltered place there to build a nest. You can make sure there is always something for birds to eat and drink.

Winter bird cake

1 In winter, there is less food for birds to find. Use breadcrumbs from a stale loaf, uncooked peanuts, bacon rind and lard to make a winter bird cake.

2 Line a cake tin or muffin tray with greaseproof paper. Now mix the breadcrumbs, peanuts and chopped bacon rind together in a bowl.

3 Lard will hold the cake together, as well as give the birds fat to eat to keep them warm. Melt the lard in a saucepan over a low heat until it is all liquid.

5 Leave the mixture to cool. Then turn it out of the tray and put your winter cake outside, out of reach of cats. Put out water too.

4 Stir the melted lard into the dry mixture and pour it into the cake tin or muffin tray.

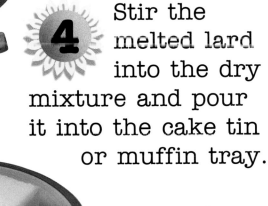

Bird food

Birds will find things to eat all over the garden.

Some birds feed on berries and fruit. Some catch insects in the air.

Caterpillars, snails and worms make a juicy meal.

Small birds peck for seeds and insects on the ground.

In winter, when the ground is hard and there are no berries, birds will eat your winter cake.

Footprints

Birds are not the only visitors to the garden who come looking for food and water. Other shy creatures come at night or when there is no one around. Their footprints will let you know who called.

Hungry visitors

1 Fill a baking tray with damp sand and smooth it over. Put food scraps like brown bread, fruit, vegetables and nuts on a plate. Pour milk or water into a saucer.

2 Put the food and liquid onto the baking tray and leave it in a quiet part of the garden. Check the tray for footprints in the morning and again in the evening.

3 Make a note of who has left tracks in the sand. Did they come at night or during the day? Look carefully, then smooth over the sand.

Identifying tracks

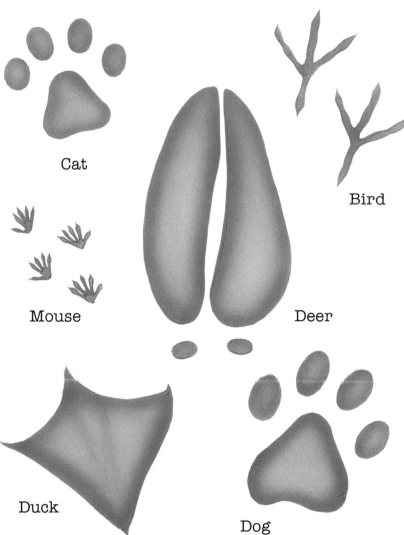

You can use these pictures to identify the footprints that have been made in your tray. These pictures are the same size as real animal footprints.

Cat

Bird

Mouse

Deer

Duck

Dog

If you can't see a print to match the ones in your tray, try to find the one that looks most like it. Can you tell if it is a bird or an animal? Is it big or small? Ask an adult to help you work out what any mystery prints are. You could look them up in a field guide.

Insects

Look for insects in the soil, under stones, on plants, resting on walls, hiding in cracks or swimming in water. Make a chart of the insects that live in or visit the garden.

Insect visitors

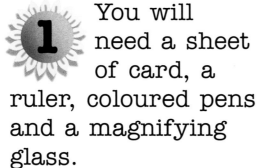

1 You will need a sheet of card, a ruler, coloured pens and a magnifying glass.

2 Copy the chart in the picture onto your card. You can add extra columns. Draw a moon if you spot an insect like a moth at night.

Where insects live

	Ladybird	Wasp	Butterfly
			x
	x		

3 Look for insects in the garden. Mark a cross on the chart to show what they are feeding on. Which part of the garden has the most visitors? Do the insects come during the day or at night?

A bug's bits

Insects all have six legs. They have a skeleton on the outside of their body and sensitive feelers called antennae. Many have wings.

Wasp

Thorax

Wing

Abdomen

Leg

Antenna

Compound eye

Insects can look very different from each other. Beetles have hard, shiny cases to protect their delicate wings. The easiest way to tell if a creature is an insect is to count its legs.

Beetle

Minibeasts

There are many small creatures, such as spiders and slugs, which are not insects. Spiders spin silky webs to catch their food. Slugs and snails slither along on silvery trails. Millipedes scuttle in dark, damp places. Set a trap to catch some minibeasts in your nature garden.

Setting a trap

1 Dig a hole in the soil just deep enough to hold a small container. Put in pieces of fruit and a spoonful of cat food or dog food.

2 Cover the trap with a small rock, propping up one end with a stone to leave a small gap.

3 Leave the trap overnight. Lift the rock to see what you have caught. Before you let your minibeasts go, try to find out what they are.

Minibeast spotting

Use a magnifying glass to see if you can spot some of these creatures in your nature garden.

A snail hides inside its shell when danger is about.

Snail

Spiders are not insects because they have eight legs.

Spider

Millipedes with hundreds of legs eat leaves and dead plants.

Millipede

Slugs come out to look for food after a shower of rain.

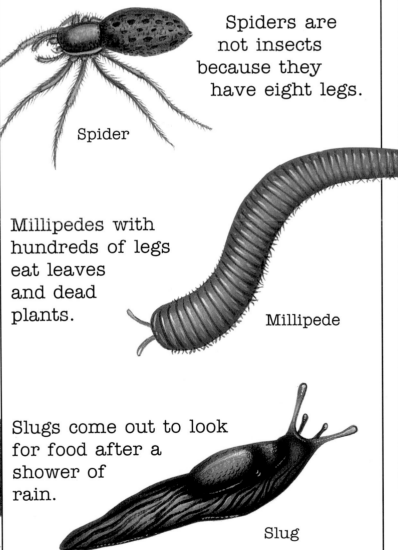

Slug

Ants

Ants have six legs, so you know they are insects. Ants often move around in long trails, following the same path. This project will help you find out if there is a busy ants' nest in your nature garden.

Ant trails

1 Mix two teaspoons of sugar in a bowl half filled with warm water. Stir until the sugar dissolves.

Bait

Bait

Nest

2 Add small pieces of stale bread and leave them to soak for a few moments. Remove the bread before it goes too soggy and take it into the garden.

Bait

3 Put pieces of bread all over the garden as bait. Ants will find the food and carry it off, moving in a line. If you follow the line, you will find the ants' nest.

4 Draw a map of where you put the bread bait. Put in lines to show the paths the ants took to carry their food. The nest should be where all the lines meet.

Bait

Bait

Ants' nests

Ants live and work together in a nest underground. They build lots of tunnels. A queen ant lays eggs. Worker ants look for food and bring it back home along the tunnels.

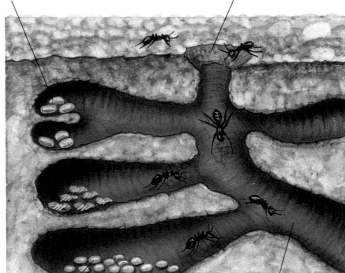

Older eggs

Entrance to nest

Young eggs

Main tunnel

Worms

As worms burrow along under the ground, they eat soil, leaving behind mounds of fine soil called worm casts. You can watch worms pull leaves and dead plants down into the soil to munch.

Worm watching

1 You will need a shoe box, a bin liner, sticky tape, clingfilm, leaves and dead plants, soil and worms.

2 Line the box with the bin liner and fix it in place with tape. This will make the box waterproof.

3 Fill the box with damp soil and put in some worms you have dug up from the soil in the garden.

4 Let the worms burrow down into the soil, then sprinkle on the plants and leaves.

5 Cover the box with clingfilm punched with holes to let in air. How long does it take for the leaves and plants to disappear?

Words on worms

Worms are not garden pests. Gardeners are very happy to have worms in the soil because they help to break it up.
Breaking up the soil keeps it full of air, which is good for growing plants.
Soil without any worms in it is solid, very heavy to dig and not as good for growing things.

Glossary

Ants

Ants are insects that live in a nest underground. They carry food away in long trails.

Turn to pages 26-27 to find out how you can lay a food trail to see if there is an ants' nest in the garden.

Birds

Birds feed on berries and fruit or insects and creatures they find on the ground. In winter, it is hard for them to find enough to eat.

You can learn how to make a winter bird cake on pages 18-19.

Decomposers

Decomposers are creatures or plants that help animals and dead plants to break down, or decompose.

You can find out how long different objects take to decompose in the project on pages 8-9.

Flowers

Flowers are where the seeds for new plants are made. They come in all shapes and sizes, but all have the same parts.

Find out what the parts of a flower are on pages 16-17.

Grass

Grass holds the soil in place and provides food for animals. Grass needs sunlight to stay green.

See how to prove that grass needs sunlight to stay green on pages 12-13.

Insects

All insects have six legs. Any creature with more or fewer than six legs is not an insect. Different insects like to feed in different places.

Chart the best places to spot insects in the garden, and look at the parts that make up an insect on pages 22-23.

Photosynthesis

Photosynthesis is the name for the way that plants use sunlight, carbon dioxide, water and the green colour in their leaves, called chlorophyll, to make their own food.

Look at how photosynthesis works on pages 12-13.

Roots

Roots hold plants firmly in the ground. Water and minerals go up through the roots and into the plant from the soil.

You can watch how plants take up water in the project on pages 14-15, using a celery stick and some coloured water.

Seeds

Plants grow from seeds. Inside a seed is a new plant and the food that it needs to begin to grow.

You can discover if there are seeds waiting to grow under the soil in the project on pages 10-11.

Soil

Soil is made up of several layers of rock and dead plants and animals that have been broken down over many years. Different types of rock break down to make different kinds of soil.

You can look at how to shake up soil so that you can see all the layers in the project on pages 6-7.

Worms

Worms live in the soil. They break up the soil and make it easier for plants to grow. Most gardeners like to have worms in their garden.

You can learn how to build your own worm garden in the project on pages 28-29.

Index